An Upside Down Tale Of

Angels, Asses, Assassins and A Baby In A Manger

Christmas: A Miscellany

Alison J. Askew

ISBN   978-1-80369-529-7

www.newgeneration-publishing.com

New Generation Publishing

Contents

Preface and Dedication

This small book is dedicated to the Christians, the Living Stones, of the Bethlehem area. It is written in gratitude for their faithfulness and friendship.

In spite of the many difficulties caused by occupation, oppression, marginalisation and financial hardship they remain resilient and joyful, taking immense pride in the fact that they live where Jesus was born. Many of them feel it is a sacred calling to remain in the Holy land rather than emigrate to a much easier life abroad.

I am particularly grateful to my Christian friends in Beit Sahour for their generosity and hospitality over many years: Nariman and George Qumsiyeh and Ibrahim Hannouneh, all members of The Orthodox Church of the Forefathers, Beit Sahour and Samer Hanna the 'Mosaic Man of Beit Sahour' of the Aramaic Church in Bethlehem. My friendship with Najwah Sahhar the amazing and inspirational powerhouse behind Jeel al Amal (Generation of Hope) a home for needy boys and co-educational school in Bethany goes back many years. I am so grateful for her friendship and her tireless commitment to the wellbeing of needy Palestinian children.

The royalties from the sale of this book are being donated to The Friends of The Holy Land providing food, medical care, education and vocational training for the neediest Christians in The Holy Land, enabling them to remain in their land and the land of Jesus.

To learn more about the work of FHL please visit their website at www.friendsoftheholyland.org.uk

I would also like to thank several good friends who made the publication of this book possible. Steve Patton for his enthusiasm for the project, putting my disorganised writings into the correct order and tidying up my mistakes; Rose Moulton who undertook the laborious task of proof reading and Canon Michael Glanville-Smith who encouraged me to write it in the first place. I would also like to thank Michael for the ongoing help, support and friendship he offers to my Mum and me and for his commitment to the people of Palestine.

I am grateful to everyone at New Generation Publishing for their help and professionalism in the production of this book.

FRIENDS OF THE HOLY LAND

FHL

GIVING HOPE TO VULNERABLE CHRISTIANS

3

Introduction

There have been many books written about Christmas: Theological books; devotional books; books exploring the traditions associated with Christmas, books offering advice as to how best to prepare for Christmas. This brief book doesn't attempt to do any of these things.

It will not offer the reader any new knowledge or fresh advice. I hope, however, it may perhaps provide new insights and fresh ways of engaging with the familiar Christmas story by approaching it from a different, slightly off centre angle. Some of the short pieces are somewhat tongue in cheek: they are not intended to cause offence or be irreverent, simply to challenge some of our popular and comfortable interpretations and practices.

The book is not aimed at the serious theologian or preacher nor the accomplished spiritual contemplative (although I hope there will be flashes of theology and spirituality along the way). Rather it is really for 'Ordinary Christians' in the pew, or those who whilst not attending church, have an interest in and feel an affinity with the Christmas story.

The pieces are deliberately short and self-contained: they are not intended to be deep or erudite. I hope they will prove to be 'Reader Friendly' and will awaken in those who read them a fresh engagement with the Christmas story and how we celebrate this amazing birth when 'The Word became flesh and dwelt among us.'

The Bible contains two distinct accounts of Jesus' birth, one as it were from Mary's perspective and one from Joseph's.
Before reading the reflections please read the Biblical accounts

Luke1:5 - 2:38 and Matthew1:18 - 2:23

1. It wasn't supposed to be like this...
Reflections for Christmas

The problem with the Christmas story is we know it too well and everyone else thinks they know it very well. We've been brought up with it; school nativity plays with the regulation checked tea towel head dresses and wet-eyed parents looking lovingly at their children who've forgotten their lines as the whole school hall is transported back to Bethlehem 2,000 years ago. Shopping is accompanied by the sound of ubiquitous carols. When did 'I'm dreaming of a White Christmas', 'Rudolph the Red-nosed Reindeer' and Slade's 'Here it is Merry Christmas' become carols?

Although robins, snowmen and Christmas trees are the most common designs on Christmas cards, those who persevere, who look, and perhaps more importantly ask, will find Mary, Joseph and the infant Jesus perhaps with a smattering of shepherds and wise men thrown in for good measure, in a place somewhat out of view like a dirty magazine. The rationale? They really don't sell that well! But perhaps that is true to the story. At the birth of Jesus, the holy family were not where anyone would have expected them to be, nor where anyone would have gone looking for them. They were out of sight and out of mind.

In our multicultural society children know the stories from all the major religions, they learn about a multitude of religious festivals. Was it Jesus or Mohammed who was born in Bethlehem and are Christmas and Divali the same thing?

Many people say it's a nice story, a baby being born in a stable surrounded by the warmth of animals but why is it such a big deal? Why do we remember the child of Bethlehem and celebrate his birth? What makes him so special? Few people in our affluent so called Christian society are particularly keen to find out. But we will put up Christmas trees, lights and decorations in his honour and wonder where he is.

If for a while we stepped outside the warmth of our safe, cosy, insulated houses and exposed ourselves to the colder more precarious world outside we might just find him. It will be hard to see him round the table groaning with more food than anyone can eat, but we may find him in the Crisis or Salvation Army centres where the Christmas fayre offered to the neediest in our land will be the best meal they've had in months. If we venture further we may detect his presence in the teenage girl who has run away from an abusive household for whom Christmas day will be spent huddled up in her trackie bottoms and a hoodie in the doorway of a shop she could never afford to buy anything from. The highlight of her Christmas is the gift of a fag from a passing stranger who feels sorry for her as he rushes to catch the train home to his family. We may see him in the psychiatric patients abandoned by their families over the festive season; they can't take up the psychiatrist's offer of a day at home over Christmas because their families are afraid of the embarrassment and the disruption they might cause at their respectable celebrations. We may find him in the old lady dying alone on the busy hospital ward because the hospital was understaffed and there was no one free to sit with her in her dying moments. If we went to the asylum processing centres where we see the world's vulnerable and desperate people who have used all their financial and emotional resources in an attempt to escape persecution in their own countries, left to sleep in overcrowded conditions and treated with indignity whilst their appeals are being processed, perhaps we might see Jesus in the refugee there. When we see the The Big Issue seller remaining polite and trying to retain hope after being verbally abused for the umpteenth time and smiling through the repetitive, hollow mantra 'Sorry I haven't got any change' don't we catch glimpses of Joseph being turned away from all the inns in Bethlehem as he tries to find shelter for his heavily pregnant wife and himself?

Perhaps we need to momentarily leave behind the cosy world of Christmas we have created with its soothing carols; glittering lights; generous but unnecessary presents and overindulgence, because Christmas was never meant to be like this and we will find it hard to encounter the child of Bethlehem there.

If we had written the Christmas story it would have been very different. There would have been far more glitz and glamour, respectability and riches. It would have been like something out of Hello magazine. The key players would certainly not have been a needy unmarried couple who couldn't find anywhere for their child to be born. His first visitors would not have been a bunch of dirty, ragged shepherds who were looked down on by respectable society who came running straight from the fields without even time to get washed and tidied up. The not so wise, wise men, would not have had to ask directions from a murderous king. We would have written it very differently making sure the unsavoury characters and unprepossessing places were airbrushed out. It would have been an altogether more respectable, glamorous and impressive story with the great and the good centre stage and a host of paparazzi catching every shiny moment.

But that wasn't the way God wanted to write His story because He isn't that kind of God.

God still comes among us in unexpected ways and in unfamiliar places. As the carol puts it 'Where meek souls will receive him, still the dear Christ enters in.'

2. Popularists or Purists?

Should we show restraint and patience and wait until later or should we just enjoy the present moment to the full like everyone else does?

No, I'm not talking about sex before marriage, but carols before Christmas.

How much does it matter that we keep two entirely separate seasons, Advent and Christmas? In the church's observance they have a very different feel. Four weeks of purple and no flowers, and if not strict fasting at least a degree of restraint, followed by a period of gold or white vestments and unfettered feasting and rejoicing. Four weeks of penitence, spiritual preparation and looking forward followed on Christmas Day by a season of celebrating the 'nowness' of our faith. God has come to us in Jesus, born as a baby in Bethlehem, He has become Immanuel, God with us.

Of course, for non-churchgoers Advent is a mystery, an unnecessary invention of the church to add to its already substantial catalogue of 'Feel Bad' offerings. Cold draughty church buildings, hard seats, long and often boring sermons a disproportionate emphasis on sin and now a sober reflection on The Four last Things – death, judgement, Heaven and Hell. Hardly 'Tidings of comfort and joy', in fact the singing of the carols that might have lifted the mood are banned until Christmas. If Father Christmas has been making appearances up and down the country since the end of October, if Christmas lights have been switched on for several weeks lighting up people's lives and lifting their spirits on cold, dark evenings, what's wrong with a few renditions of carols in December?

Wouldn't you have thought that the church would be grateful that the largely secular world actually wants to sing the songs that tell of the birth of God's son and that the good news is for all people? Is the church just showing itself in a negative, petulant and judgmental fashion, making a fuss over nothing? Why spoil people's joy; after all wasn't Jesus himself big on joy and celebration and enhancing people's lives rather than erecting barriers and rules? If people don't get Advent but want to celebrate Christmas albeit a bit early, why not encourage them? What's the problem?

But could it be there is another side to this? Could Advent have its own important and distinctive value that we should safeguard rather than consigning to the archives of irrelevance?

We live in a world that seeks and expects instant results and instant gratification. We don't expect to have to wait. We want something and we want it now. Fast food, instant replies to emails, buying things online with a click. Gone are the days of waiting for good food rather than quick food, waiting with a sense of excitement for a letter in the post, perusing things in a shop, making a choice and then having to queue to pay. No, all too time consuming. And yet, aren't we somehow the poorer for our rushed, pressured lifestyles. Isn't it true that often we appreciate things more when we have to wait for them? A time of waiting may be no bad thing.

Our society tells us we can have whatever we want because we're worth it. We have become increasingly hedonistic. For many people there is little differentiation between what they want and what they think they need. Special has become ordinary and so we no longer appreciate things. Isn't there an argument for times of fasting or at least moderation in order that times of feasting really are special and occasions of celebration?

Most people are worn out at the end of Christmas Day so perhaps we do need the slower pace, the time for reflection that Advent offers us so that we don't just rush through Christmas without actually celebrating anything other than our survival of it.

3. Christmas: It's for the children, isn't it?

How many times have I heard people say this and each time I want to cry out and say 'No, it's not just for children, it's for everyone, but maybe they can help us to appreciate it better and enter into the spirit of it'.

Isn't it sad that many adults feel so embarrassed and uncomfortable with the celebration of Christmas and all that it stands for that they want to dissociate themselves from it, 'Of course we only do it for the kids'. They feel that if they said they enjoyed the celebration of the birth of Jesus; that it put them in touch with a time of innocence and inner joy; that they actually valued entering into the realm of mystery and wonder, then they would be derided and would lose their street cred. Surely belief in Christmas is for the gullible and the needy.

Of course, most of us ditched Father Christmas long before year six of primary school – the mince pie and the glass of sherry that had always been consumed by daybreak; the visit of the old man with the bushy beard magically brought on his sleigh by reindeer even when it wasn't snowing; the rotund man actually getting down the chimney and finding alternative ways of beneficent house-breaking in the post coal fire era – it really was all rather fanciful. But when we ditch Father Christmas don't we also, often, throw the baby out with the bath water? The particular baby in question being the one born in a stable at Bethlehem.

How have we got to a place where we find a sense of mystery, of otherness, of excitement and undiluted joy to be childish things, things that we should grow out of? The older we get the more cynical and sceptical we become: Christmas is not for cynics and sceptics. Christmas is for those who can still believe in a message of peace and goodwill; Christmas is for those who can still, however distantly, hear the song of the angels, Christmas is for those who still have the capacity to experience joy and delight. If that is all childish stuff then maybe Christmas is only for children after all, or perhaps Christmas teaches us that we need to become like little children.

Children can teach us how to enjoy Christmas, how to appreciate the world better; children can teach us not to take ourselves too seriously; children help us to live in the present moment without being distracted by worries about tomorrow.

God created a world that was good, lovely and beautiful; a world he wanted us to enjoy, but we make it all too serious, too difficult, too competitive, anxiously guarding what we think is ours and making sure no-one gets their grubby little hands on it.

Look at children's faces when they see the light on the Christmas tree, when they rip the paper off a present, when they look out of the window and see that it's snowing – pure unadulterated joy: the joy of the moment, spontaneous and genuine. But when we get older we see the same sources of joy through different eyes. We look at the mess the Christmas tree will make when it sheds its needles, we look at the child's present knowing that it may get broken or forgotten and regret how much it cost, we think of the inconvenience the snow will cause. We have created a world where we expect problems.

We need Christmas to help us relearn how to share in the joy that was the creator's plan; to enjoy without feeling guilty or self-conscious. To learn to laugh at things, even the most ridiculous of Christmas cracker jokes; to learn to appreciate the effort people went to in sending a card (particularly given the cost of a stamp), to value the thought behind the gift and the intention of the giver rather than dismissing it as not really our kind of thing and putting it on one side for the next tombola. We need to invite people round for a drink not out of a sense of obligation but out of a sense of generosity and goodwill; to learn how to laugh at the childish silliness of wearing a paper crown without having to be fueled by alcohol first.

Children appreciate Christmas; they love every aspect of it. As we get older and allegedly wiser, we lose the enjoyment, some even come to dread it: the expense, the busyness, the preparations, all the self- imposed social expectations that we feel obliged to take on board.

Why can't we just rejoice in the amazing truth that God, the creator of all things chose to be born as a baby in Bethlehem, that He chose and chooses to live amongst us, that He wants us to enjoy and delight in His creation?

Perhaps we need a child to take us by the hand and lead us to the party!

4. Words

I love words, they fascinate me.
They offer an endless choice of possibilities and combinations.
Words are a precious resource to be used respectfully and with due consideration,
yet most of the time they are trivialized and devalued.
In a hasty, thoughtless 'one word will do as well as another' society, we prefer text friendly abbreviations and emojis to words.
But words matter.
The words we use and the words we choose not to use.
How we use them, how often we use them.
The order in which we use them.
The space between the words; the words unspoken.
The words implied but not overtly stated.
How we use words reveals something important about us.
The extent of our vocabulary.
Whether we are an analytical or a creative, imaginative thinker.
Do we want to shock? Do we want to please?
Do we want to be understood or do we want to confound the reader or listener?
Words well used linger in our memories and our consciousness long after they've been read or heard.
Words change things, sometimes forever.
'I love you', 'I hate you'.
'Guilty', 'innocent', 'I now pronounce you man and wife'.
Words have a power greater than the combination of the vowels and consonants in them.
Words have a life, they are dynamic.

The Word became flesh and dwelt among us.

Profound, paradoxical stuff, but that is the punchline of the prologue of St John's gospel.
That is the punchline of the entire gospel.

The word. Which word? THE WORD.
The ultimate word. God's communication of Himself.
God's self-revelation.
The word, that which when spoken, when commanding, brought all created things into being.
The word that is the reason, the logic, the meaning and the purpose underlying everything.
The word that is the foundation upon which every other form of communication is based.
The spoken word communicated by the prophets.
The written word enshrined in scripture.
The word was not abstract, not a concept but living, dynamic, creative and life changing.
This word, which was God, became human.
He communicated with us in the words, the only language we could comprehend.
The Word became flesh and dwelt among us.
He got on our wavelength and used our language.
He didn't use a foreign language, the language of heaven
But used our language, the language of earth.
He became incarnate, enfleshed, and lived among us as one of us.

It's here that Saint John begins his gospel in the juxtaposition between time and eternity,
The intersection of heaven and earth which coalesced in The Word becoming flesh
A unique, unrepeatable, word defying, world changing event.

Matthew and Luke both begin their gospels with the birth of a baby and the angelic preparations for that birth,

Mark begins with the call to repentance but John is not
merely concerned with narrative,
His interest is in the meaning behind the storyline,
The Word behind the words.
The rest all follows on from this profound truth 'The Word
became flesh and dwelt among us... full of grace and truth'

The Word beyond words, the word too big for our words,
The word that strains our words to breaking point,
The Word uttered from all eternity to all eternity.

All the rest is His story.

5. The Prophet

You have a saying 'Hindsight is a wonderful thing'.
I like to think foresight is also a wonderful thing.
I was a prophet. You'll be familiar with much that I wrote,
Although actually, it wasn't all me, there were three of us
living at different times,
But our messages got combined and attributed to one person.
However, that's not important,
Who wrote what doesn't really matter,
For the words were God's not ours.

You may think being a prophet is a glamorous calling,
Let me tell you nothing could be further from the truth.
It was a costly vocation.
Delivering messages people didn't want to hear,
Telling them things they didn't believe,
Speaking out against what was wrong in society and religion.
We were not popular, harsh punishments were not
uncommon.
The problem is when you declare a prophecy people want
all the detail-
When, where, how will it all happen?
In my experience most prophecies tend to be quite vague on
those details,
So, of course in your own lifetime it was hard to see whether
you had been right or not,
Whether you were a genuine man of God or a charlatan.
But sometimes there were beautiful, wonderful messages
About God doing amazing things in the future.
Prophecies about a virgin being with child,
A glorious future of peace, stability and goodwill.
The great thing was the original prophecies were added to,
Given more credibility by the ones that followed,
It was like lots of pieces of a jigsaw all coming together.

Of course, I never lived to see it all come true,
And yet it did come true, God sent His Messiah,
Born of a virgin, to usher in an age of peace,
To establish God's kingdom on earth.

Sometimes the prophets had to work hard to find the words,
But other times they just flowed from the pen, word for word,
Fully formed in beautiful poetry or prose.
I still get a sense of joy when I hear those words read each
year at your carol services….
I knew they were true, they stood the test of time.
Such clear and unusual pictures, we could never have made
them up.

A branch springing from the root of Jesse, God's spirit
resting upon him;
A spirit of wisdom and understanding, of counsel and of power.
Someone who would judge the poor with justice,
Not something I often experienced in my lifetime.
Someone who would defend the humble with equity- how
different the world would be.
Even the world of nature would live at peace,
Wolves and lambs; leopards and kids, calves and young lions,
Those not normally bedfellows would lie down together,
A picture beyond human imagining.
No hurt or harm, how wonderful, how miraculous.
This vision, this hope, this promise was something to hang onto
In the world of injustice, conflict and tribulation.

And there was the prophecy to bring comfort to God's people,
The clearing of a road in the wilderness; the raising of valleys,
The levelling of mountains.
Good news 'The Lord is here',
How beautiful on the mountains are the feet of the herald
Who brings good news, who announces deliverance.
Wonderful poetic words. Words we could never have created.

Did we fully understand what we were saying?
No, because we lived in very different times to the ones we were describing,
And yet we felt compelled to prophesy, to speak out,
To announce God's new future.
It all came to fruition many years later and not in the way we would have predicted.

All our beautiful words were pointing forward
To the birth of a baby in a stable at Bethlehem.
To the proclamation of God's kingly rule and the breaking in of his kingdom.

Yet still we wait for its final realisation.
The king came, the promises were fulfilled, but the Kingdom wasn't accepted, it was too radical.
The world still needs prophets.

6. The Archangel Gabriel

You will have heard of me and no doubt my companions, and members of the other heavenly orders, but I don't want you to get bogged down with the details of who we all are and what we do.

I want to share with you a remarkable memory I have about a time so long ago: actually, when you live and work in the context of eternity, time becomes rather a meaningless concept, but that's another digression. I had been in God's presence doing His will for as long as I can remember, certainly long before the creation of your earth, although clearly I hadn't been there for all eternity as that is only true of God Himself.

I had watched with interest the development of your world which God had created in His love; so much beauty and variety, such endless possibilities, no wonder he was pleased with what He'd made and called it good. My chief fascination was when He created you human beings in His own image, just a little lower than the angels. As time went on the human race multiplied and as he told them inhabited the earth and subdued it, although their understanding of what that meant wasn't what He had in mind..... Strange and sad that having being made in His image, created in love and declared to be very good, they should so often seem entirely dissimilar to Him, not showing His likeness at all. But of course some of them loved Him, walked with Him and did good things for others; some like Him, created things of beauty or showed undeserved acts of kindness and

21

generosity. Beautiful and impressive cities grew up and the earth became what you would call civilized.

Anyhow, to cut a very long story short, because I know you couldn't cope with the wide horizons of eternity or the unlimited joys of Heaven, after a longer amount of time than you could get your heads round, He called me to go on a very special mission for Him. I'd done God's bidding for aeons but this was really the first time I questioned what He had in mind. Although this sounds totally outrageous, I even questioned His wisdom and His judgement. He asked me to go to your little planet, to a small, insignificant town called Nazareth, to a young woman who was engaged to a man called Joseph, and tell her that she was to have a special son, born in a unique way, not through human conception but through the overshadowing of The Holy Spirit. So far so good. Of course God can perform miracles He's performed more miracles than, what's your phrase, 'You've had hot dinners'. God can do far more than you could imagine because He is God. No, it wasn't the nature of the birth that I had to announce that was the problem, it was just about everything else associated with God's idea and the message I had to deliver.

No disrespect, but why your little planet? There are bigger brighter ones, although He always had a special fondness for yours after he'd created your forebears in his image. But having chosen your earth why in Heaven's name Nazareth? It was a backwater, not well known for anything, it had no famous sons or daughters. Frankly if I was planning a special mission with a pretty stunning message I'd have chosen somewhere a bit more impressive than Nazareth to be the setting of the first part of the story.

If I was to go to earth why not Rome or Jerusalem, great cities so I'm told, but no, it was to be Nazareth. It was also a very ordinary house I was directed to. Not that I'm a heavenly snob but I do sometimes wonder at God's taste. Anyhow, who am I to question His judgement? I'm here to do His bidding not question it and so off I went on the first leg of my mission.

I have to say I was more than pleasantly surprised. The young woman to whom I was sent, Mary, was quite remarkable. I had a message which it would have been hard for anyone to believe. I told her God had chosen her to be mother of His son with all that that entailed. The poor girl wasn't even married. I could well imagine the ridicule and rejection she'd experience when she tried to tell people she was bearing God's son. But Mary seemed unfazed. Her reply was that if this was God's will then she was putting herself at His disposal. It was truly a privilege to meet her, some journeys stay in my mind forever and of course, as always, God knew what He was doing.

That taught me an important lesson. It's not the big or impressive things that are valuable, it's not the important and influential people that are precious to God but the simple people of faith who trust His promises and make themselves available to share in His loving purposes. So, a journey I had thought was a waste of time and an error of judgement on God's part was a source of great joy and enlightenment to me not to mention the way it changed the course of your human history.

7. Elizabeth

It's strange isn't it, you wait all your life for a baby and then out of the blue two come almost at once from nowhere.

Let me explain. My name is Elizabeth, I'm an old woman, I'm married to Zechariah, an old man, one of the priests who serve in the temple in Jerusalem. He's a good man, he takes his religious duties seriously and we've had a long and happy marriage except we were never blessed with the gift of children. I won't pretend that hasn't been hard, it has been like a cloud hanging over us. Rejoicing with other people at the birth of their children and grandchildren just reminds us of what we've missed out on.

Everyone believes children are a gift from God, a sign of His blessing and pleasure, so when a couple can't have children, questions are always asked as to why, have they sinned against God? Of course, it's much worse for poor Zechariah; when he went to the temple the other priests would mutter amongst themselves, discreetly of course, but he always knew they were talking about us and asking why we had no children. Was Zechariah perhaps not as holy as he seemed, or had he married a less than suitable wife?

For many years we'd hoped and prayed for a child, but there comes a point in life when however strong your faith you realise things will never change, the family name will not be continued. We'd reached that point long ago and whilst still saddened we'd resigned ourselves to what must be.

For all our faith we had underestimated God. We'd forgotten that He isn't limited to our understanding of how things work. God has a way of surprising, even shocking people. And so it was with us. I know appearances of angels and barren old women having children don't happen, but in our case they did. And there's the parallel story of my young relative Mary, but more of that later.

It all started in the temple, as good a place as any. Zechariah was performing his priestly duties as he had done so many times before, but this was to be the day that our lives changed forever and we got caught up in God's blessing. When he came home from the temple from his period of duty I was so concerned about him; he couldn't speak, he seemed in a state of shock. I thought he'd had a stroke or something similar, and yet he was smiling. Not the smile of someone who is out of touch with reality, but the smile of a man at peace, the smile of a man who has experienced something amazing or heard wonderful news. He tried to a gesticulate what had happened it was like a serious version of charades. And wonder of wonders, I conceived and as they say, 'I was with child'. Our prayers had been answered, our disgrace removed. How I praised God and thanked Him for His goodness.

But can you believe it, that wasn't the end of the blessings. Even before my special, God given son was born I heard that my young relative Mary was herself pregnant. Her story was as miraculous as mine. She too had had an unexpected visit from the angel Gabriel. I should say, Mary is a very devout, respectable girl, but the angel Gabriel said she was going to have a son. Naturally she a virgin was incredulous, such things don't happen. But apparently the angel wasn't to be discouraged. Mary would have a child because she would be overshadowed by the Holy Spirit and the child would be called the Son of God. What rejoicing in our family!

It wasn't long after Mary received the amazing news that she came to visit me. What joy we had to share, what stories we had to tell about God's graciousness. What hopes and dreams, we both knew we were blessed, we had been called to be part of God's great story. People would talk about us as we had talked about Hannah and her special son Samuel.

I was so pleased to see Mary. Our joy knew no bounds as we shared a long and tight embrace and began to share our stories. That was the first time our sons 'met' each other and can you believe it, though yet unborn, they somehow recognized each other. The child in my womb leapt for joy in the presence of his unborn relative. My joy was only surpassed when my son was born. It was only then that poor old Zechariah got his speech back as he wrote down that, in spite of expectations and tradition our son would not be named after his father but would be called John.

With hindsight I can say that was only the beginning of the story, God's story. Who'd have thought that Mary and I, the most unlikely of Jewish mothers would have sons who were divinely given, divinely inspired and who would play their unique roles in the history of our people and the entire world.

Never in my wildest dreams would I have thought such a thing could happen. It just goes to show, don't underestimate God.

8. The Inn Keeper

There are some people you never forget. That little family falls into that category.

Their faces remain etched in my memory.

There was nothing exceptional about them apart from their circumstances.

For them it was a question of being in the wrong place at the wrong time.

It was mayhem; an administrative disaster.

One of the unpopular, unnecessary moves by the Roman authorities just to remind us they were in control, and they could make our lives difficult simply by issuing an edict.

The emperor had the bright idea of holding a census.

No doubt the idea was to check that everyone was paying their taxes and that people knew they were being monitored.

The plan was everyone had to return to their place of origin to be registered there.

As you can imagine, the roads were busy, people travelling hither and thither.

It was inconvenient and costly.

When they'd arrived in their ancestral home often after days of travelling, they had to find somewhere to stay.

Here in Bethlehem it was very much a case of demand outstripping supply.

Of course, those who were young and fit arrived early and secured the best accommodation,

For those who arrived later it was pot luck.

But that poor couple arrived too late even for a basic, bottom of the range room somewhere.

When they arrived at my door they were utterly exhausted And she was on the verge of giving birth.

They had come all the way from Nazareth, a long, wearisome journey.
I wondered how they'd even managed to get here.
The Roman rules made no allowances for the elderly, the infirm or the heavily pregnant,
All had to make the journey to be registered,
Kindness and compassion didn't feature in the policy.
When I saw their longing faces, the desperation in their eyes, their exhaustion,
My heart sank.
You see I had a guest room, but it had been let out long ago, paid for up front.
The people in it were the fussy kind who are not easily pleased, who will always find something wrong.
I simply couldn't ask them to move out although everything in me wanted to,
And yet I couldn't turn away the couple from my door either.
My wife always says I'm too soft for my own good, but there they were two desperate human beings, a long way from home and nowhere to stay through no fault of their own.
I hadn't got a room for them, but I could offer them the stable under the house.
It wasn't much, but it was all that I had, better that than sending them on their way thinking the poor girl would give birth in a hedgerow somewhere.
It suddenly struck me how awful it must be to be without shelter a long way from home,
To be totally vulnerable and helpless.
I was embarrassed and apologetic to offer them the stable, but they responded as if I'd offered them a five star hotel.
At once the anxiety and desperation fell from their faces, their shoulders visibly relaxed.
I was so pleased to have been able to offer something however humble and inadequate.
If nothing else, the stable was safe and warm, it would protect them from the elements.

They could lay down on matting and the straw and the baby when it was born could be placed in the manger a snug, makeshift crib.

I took them down to their overnight stay and tried to make it as welcoming as possible.

I apologized for the presence of the animals, but the man looked at me and said 'It's their home, we're the ones that should be apologizing for disturbing them. They'll be welcome company'.

After that I said I'd leave them to have some privacy; they certainly wouldn't want me around when the poor lady gave birth.

I promised I'd drop in later to check all was well and ask if they needed anything.

When I did return what a picture.

Such joy and tenderness in the eyes of the young mother, such protection and pride on the face of the older man, and the baby exuded utter contentment, smiling wide eyed from the warm straw in the manger.

I could see all was well; they looked completely at home in my animals' shelter.

The animals too looked on the family with a calm acceptance and benevolence as if they somehow knew they had witnessed something extraordinary and were glad to have shared their home with this human family.

I often wonder what became of them.

I hope life became easier for them.

I wonder if they will ever tell people where their son was born?

I wonder what he'll grow up to be.

9. Seth the Shepherd Boy of Bethlehem

My name is Seth, not that I expect you to remember that, or even to be particularly interested. Usually when people want to call me or speak to me they just say 'Hey you, lad'. You see I'm a shepherd, to be more accurate an under shepherd. My father is a shepherd, so is my grandad, so was his father before him; it goes in the family, it's what we do.

For as long as I can remember I've been out on the hills around Bethlehem with the men, picking up their skills, their humour and their music making. It's a hard job but I'll never know another. It can be cold outside at night; it can be dangerous fending off wild animals and opportunist thieves but there is such a wonderful sense of warmth and camaraderie as we gather round a fire staring up at the inky black sky and sharing stories and singing songs. Tales of long ago, of the brave deeds of those who had gone before us.

None of us were educated, I mean why waste a good schooling on someone who was going to spend their time with sheep? We do the job the owners of the sheep don't want to do. A few of us own their own sheep but not many. We shepherds were always looked down on, held at arms' length by the people in Bethlehem and the surrounding villages. I can understand why – putting it bluntly we are not known for our personal hygiene and we smell of sheep! We can't often have a proper wash and we rarely have the time off to go back to the civilizing influence of our women folk, and of course we don't often make it to the synagogue on the Sabbath either. Sabbath rest is all well and good but sheep need feeding, watering and keeping safe on the Sabbath as much as on any other day. Shepherding really is a full time job.

I never had any ambitions beyond the Bethlehem hills. If it doesn't sound stupid, I actually love the sheep, I care about them, I've given them all names. Other people might look at them and just see a flock of indistinguishable animals but to me each one is unique, it has its own character. I love the way they follow my call or whistle, the way they trust me, and I've always tried my best never to let them down. I like the feel of their warm wool when they nuzzle up to me when they've had an accident and I rescue them, carrying them home on my shoulders. People call sheep stupid; they're not stupid they're just trusting.

It was out on the hills that I learned the ancient songs and tried my hand at writing new ones, composing simple tunes to play on my little wooden flute. I often think of David, you know, David the shepherd, the youngest son of Jesse. He was a shepherd boy here just like me. Did he sit under the same trees as me in the daytime, keeping out of the heat of the sun? Did he shelter in the same caves we do to escape the cold and chilling winds at night? Like me, he too wrote songs, but of course his are better known than mine will ever be. But he was one of us, this was his home, this was his life until he became famous and was made king. There's a lot to be proud of in being a shepherd whatever people may say.

Sitting out for hours under the night sky you have a lot of time to think, to watch, to listen, if you like to tune into the world. The old shepherds are wise men, not in the conventional way of course. They know what the weather will be like by looking at the sky, they predict the seasons, how cold or how mild it will be by observing the natural world. We have our sages who hand down the time-honoured wisdom. They may not be wise in the ways of the world but they understood the world beyond the world. They star gaze, they dream dreams, they see beyond what others see looking out into the vastness of the universe. How can you do that and not develop a sense of awe, an awareness of the mystery and wonder of what lays just out of reach?

That night I had been day dreaming (if you can do that at night), reflecting, my mind miles away. Suddenly I was aware of something which seemed totally unreal; nothing could have prepared me for it. The whole sky was illuminated and there was the sound of the most indescribably beautiful, heavenly music, which is exactly what it was. For that moment it seemed there was no distinction between heaven and earth; I was mesmerised. A choir of angels was singing right where we were and the message: Peace….. goodwill ……a baby in a manger and the saviour has been born. When one of our elders said 'Let's go to Bethlehem and see this thing that has happened' I didn't need any encouragement. It was a no brainer. Bethlehem was only a mile down the road. This was a once in a lifetime experience and I wasn't going to miss it for anything or anyone. I was off.

I certainly didn't have the longest legs but I had the quickest, and so I got to the stable first. In spite of my excitement I remembered my manners. It would have been disrespectful for me to rush in before my elders, and so, breathless, I waited for them to arrive, willing them to hurry up. After what seemed an eternity of waiting I went in with them and there was the most curious, beautiful sight, a new born baby in an animals' feeding trough, looked on by his adoring mother.

A baby is a baby whether a new born lamb or a human, helpless, vulnerable and small. It didn't look like he'd been born very long, his wet hair still sticking to his head, but there was something incredibly beautiful about him. He could only have been an hour or so old, if that, and yet he seemed full of the wisdom and experience of eternity. I can't explain it but his gaze drew me in, drew something out of me, moved me in a way that defies reason. For all my youthful excitement and normal boisterousness I fell silent and still and just gazed at him.

When we got back to our sheep that night I could scarcely believe what we had experienced. I said to my old grandad 'Why us? Why was this revealed to us, simple shepherds out of sight and out of mind?' He looked at me with his wise old eyes and smiled and said 'Why not us? Haven't you ever thought God has a wonderful sense of humour?'

10. Joseph

People often used to say to me 'Didn't you mind always being in the background,
Always a supporting actor and never the star?'
I thought that was a strange way of seeing things,
I was just being myself.
My name is Joseph, the tekton – carpenter/builder of Nazareth.
Let me tell my own story.
I was an ordinary man doing an ordinary but necessary job,
And it happened by God's grace, that I fell in love with an extraordinary young woman.
We were engaged to be married, it was to be the proudest day of my life.
Then out of the blue Mary dropped the bombshell,
She was pregnant. You could have knocked me down with a feather.
Mary, my Mary.
Mary who I'd always thought was so pure, so God fearing,
Having someone else's child.
I was hurt and disappointed beyond all expression.
But still I loved her, I wished her no ill,
I sought no retribution.
And so I did what I thought any compassionate man would have done,
I decided the marriage couldn't go ahead but she would face no consequences.
I'm not one for honour killings for enforcing the right to stone unfaithful women to death.
She was to be erased from my life without a fuss,
Sparing her as much embarrassment as possible.
Fighting back my tears I resolved not to get angry or violent.
She tried to explain to me,

She gave me a ludicrous account of where the child had come from,
I'm afraid with every goodwill in the world I wasn't going to swallow that,
But I didn't laugh at her.
Perhaps she had convinced herself of the truth of her story,
No doubt it's what she wanted me to believe too.

As I was trying to work out the best, kindest way of telling her that the wedding was off,
I had a visit from an angel in a dream,
Extraordinary but true.
Believe me I'm not a man given to imagination and supernatural happenings,
I'm down to earth, work with my hands,
I like things I can see and feel,
Wood, hammers and nails, that's always been my reality, that's what I relate to.
But contrary to all of my instincts I believed the angel.
Mary had not been unfaithful,
Her unborn son was a gift from God.
More than that, I was in on it too,
I had been called, or was it instructed, to take Mary as my wife
And by implication to take on the child too.
How do you say No to an angel particularly when they tell you something so wonderful?
Of course I could have dismissed the whole thing as vain imagining,
I could have stuck to my original plan of putting Mary away quietly.
But I committed myself to my calling as she had to hers.

I realised it wouldn't be easy,
The wagging tongues,
The disdain in which I'd be held for 'not being a man',
Not protecting my honour.

But it was the right thing to do and I've always tried to do the right thing.
I realised my life was taking on a new, unexpected turning,
I didn't know how things would work out for any of us,
But my role in God's plan was clear.
I had always taken a pride in my work,
Nothing fancy, nothing showy, just good solid, dependable work,
Door frames, chairs, tables and ploughs,
Things that were necessary in every household,
Things that were often taken for granted and seldom admired.
I was to be like my furniture.
Solid, dependable, supportive, useful, never letting anyone down.
And so it was.
I was like the door frame that held the weight,
Protecting and providing for Mary and the child.
That was the role I had been assigned.
I was happy to quietly fulfil it, living in the shadows
But always surrounded by the light.

11. The Ass

Before I tell my story I've a bone to pick with you humans
And I'd like to set the record straight.
When one of you is stupid or obstinate you describe them
as an ass.
That's inaccurate and it's an insult to the lovely donkey.
Asses are not stupid - they're gentle, obedient, humble,
uncomplaining and hardworking,
That makes them open to exploitation and mistreatment by
you humans.
Now I've got that off my chest I'll tell you my story.

I'm a donkey from Bethlehem,
The town and the fields around it are all familiar to me.
I carry loads of cut olive branches for farmers,
I take people's fruit and vegetables to the market,
I help on the land and of course I carry people.
I'm not fast but I'm reliable and sure footed,
I'm nimble and I can pick my way amongst the crowded
streets.
I work hard but I'm lucky because in the cold evenings I
come inside,
I have a warm shelter in a stable.
My story took place in that stable, my home.
It was the most curious and beautiful experience of my life.
It would have been one evening I came back from a normal
day's work-
Vegetables to the market, water to the dry hillside terraces of
land,
I'd brought back a fresh supply of straw for the stable,
I was tired but glad to be back after a busy day.
I went the manger for some hay
And would you believe it?

Snuggled into the hay was a newborn human baby.
How strange, how beautiful, this helpless little child a guest in our stable.
I looked at him in amazement,
I was glad he was there,
He looked at me and smiled.
It was a different look from the look of those who place burdens on my back,
He didn't want me to do anything,
We both just looked at each other with a love and understanding
That transcended our different ways of speaking.
He was unlike any other human I'd ever seen.
You will call me stupid, but animals sometimes have a greater insight than you humans who think you are so wise but are often blind to things you don't understand.
As I looked at that child's face, I saw something of God,
God making Himself at home in our stable,
God amongst us sharing our hospitality.
I should like to do something for that child when he grows up,
It would be a privilege to carry him: perhaps our paths will cross again.

12. A Wise Man

It was a strange story, even stranger the way history told it,
Added to it and embellished it.
First of all, just to put the record straight our names were
not Melchior, Gaspar and Balthasar,
There were not three of us and we certainly weren't kings.
As far as I'm concerned, not that I can speak for the others,
We were not particularly wise men either.
We were what you'd call searchers, seekers after the truth.
We took an interest in religions and spiritual enlightenment,
If anything we were Zoroastrians,
But the whole point was we didn't really want to be tied
down to any specific set of beliefs or practices. We were as
you'd say, somewhat eclectic.
No religion we'd ever come across really satisfied us,
All seemed to be lacking something,
But the quest for the divine light or energy was really our
motivation.
We felt fire was a symbol of the presence of the divine
It was a sign of God's conquest of darkness and evil,
So naturally we took an interest in astral bodies,
We believed they could communicate important messages
and truths about unseen realities.

We'd heard of the religion of the Jews,
An ancient religion like ours.
We admired their morality, the codes that guided their society.
We were attracted to their belief in the Messiah whom God
would send,
To right the wrongs on earth and show people God's truth.
The conviction that they were God's people,
That He cared for them in a special way had its attraction too.

We were always looking, searching,
Hoping that one day we would make a profound discovery,
That a hidden truth would be revealed to us,
Something that would lead us to the source of all things.
We were open minded,
Willing to explore, to learn from different cultures.

Then one night we saw it,
A bright new star,
Surely it signified something portentous.
We determined to study it, to discover what its message was,
For stars are signs.
For those with patience they reveal things.
When we were agreed as to its meaning we determined to
follow it.
We were sure it heralded the birth of a new king,
The king of the Jews, could 'our' star actually be telling of
the birth of the Messiah?
Clearly it took time, buying all that was necessary for a long
journey,
Making provision for our families during our absence,
And buying appropriate gifts to take one whose birth was
announced by a bright new star.
Having made our preparations we set off with a mixture of
anticipation and trepidation.
We talked on the way about gods, about good and evil,
About the way of knowledge.
We tried to imagine a world where darkness and evil had
been vanquished
Because all of this seemed to be at the heart of our journey.
Our faith in the guiding property of the star was absolute,
If it was a source of divine revelation why would we doubt it?
Eventually we arrived in Jerusalem which we knew was the
Jewish capital,
The place where they believed their God was to be
encountered in His holy temple.

It was a beautiful, impressive city, worthy of such a noble people,
And we made our way to the royal palace
For surely there we would find the new born king and our quest would be over.
Herod, the king we encountered was a nasty piece of work.
Far from welcoming us and celebrating this new birth with us he was hostile, on edge:
Something not quite right.
If we'd have been better acquainted with the Jewish scriptures
We wouldn't have needed to ask where the Messiah was to be born.
He told us it was Bethlehem, somewhere we'd never heard of.
He ordered us to locate the child and report back to him,
He too would like to pay his homage.
Strange that. Why didn't he just come with us? He could have seen for himself.
Soon it all made sense.
He was scared witless by this child.
His purpose was murder not worship.

The scene we encountered at Bethlehem was not at all what we had expected.
No palace, no splendor, nothing to dazzle or impress.
Just a baby and two very ordinary looking parents
And yet there was an unearthly splendour shining from the child.

So what did we discover? What truths were imparted to us?
That goodness and greatness are not the same thing.
That true honour is to be found in simplicity and humility.
That what is found, the thing of true and lasting worth isn't always what you were looking for.
If you don't search you won't find.
And you have to make the journey to discover what is at the end of it
And perhaps discover your true self along the way.

13. Herod

People call me xenophobic but on this occasion my mistrust of foreigners was well founded.
True, I've not got the best of reputations and I don't suffer fools gladly,
Nor do I take the risk of countenancing threats to my power.
Am I paranoid? Some say so.
I'd just say I'm careful and know I always need to watch my back.
I may seem powerful, I may rule with a rod of iron,
But opposition could come from almost any quarter.
My position is actually quite insecure.
I never know where trouble may come from- family, enemies, alleged fellow countrymen.
I always have to be vigilant, and well, do whatever is necessary to survive.
You see the bottom line is I'm not popular. I'm feared not loved.
I'm seen by some as an outsider, unworthy of being called a Jewish ruler;
The Romans treat me with suspicion even though I rule in their name;
The zealots hate me, seeing me as a traitor to the Jewish people and a collaborator with Rome, I also have an uneasy relationship with the religious authorities.

Yes, you will no doubt judge me harshly,
Say I was barbaric and that I over reacted,
But look at it through my eyes.

I was visited by a shifty group of foreigners, priests of some Persian sect,
Purporting to be astrologers, claiming they were following a star which they believed would lead them to the new-born king of the Jews.
Immediately I was propelled into pure panic mode.
King of the Jews? That's me!
I hadn't just had a son and successor. What was all of this about?
Of course, I could have dismissed them as a bunch of nutters, a company of deluded foreigners,
A group of rather second-rate astrologers who'd attached undue significance to a star,
But their intensity and the fact that they'd travelled so far made me take them seriously.

I thought my cunning, my powers of acting would outwit them,
But in the end, they got the better of me.
I feigned a deep interest in the child's birth,
I said like them, I would like to visit him and pay him homage.
The deal was when they had found him they would come and tell me,
Then of course I could dispose of him with minimal fuss.
But, like the dirty, disreputable foreigners that they were they tricked me.
They never came back and I had no idea where the child was,
This child that threatened my throne, perhaps my life.
He had to go.
But how do you remove someone when you don't know where they are or what they look like?
It suddenly became a much bigger operation than I would have wished,
But I simply couldn't afford to take any chances.
If hundreds of innocent baby boys were butchered, so be it,
So long as the guilty one was done away with.
I made my calculations and built in a generous margin of error.

All the baby boys of two years old and younger in the vicinity of Bethlehem were killed.
Not nice but necessary.
But you'll know as well as I do that politics often isn't nice.
Sometimes opponents have to be removed by whatever means.
Sometimes drastic actions have to be taken and heavy prices paid.
It will always be so.
I'm not the first and I certainly won't be the last,
Mark my word on that.

14. The Bereaved Mother

Of course, it's not his fault and I don't hold him to account,
But the reality is if he hadn't been born my son would still be
alive.
I'm one of the mothers who continue to grieve for their beloved
sons,
The Holy Innocents who were murdered by the
bloodthirsty, paranoid king Herod.
Our sons had done no wrong, their lives snuffed out before
they began to live.
Our hopes and dreams died with them,
The lost generation of Bethlehem.
We were all the victims of the mad king's fear and hatred.
There was no warning, no time to try to hide our sons, no
time to escape.
The edict was issued and suddenly there were soldiers
rampaging through the town,
Knocking down doors, barging into our homes on their
merciless quest.
Didn't those men have feelings?
Surely some of them were husbands and fathers.
But I don't blame them.
As we were afraid of them they were afraid of the mad king
whose bidding they carried out.
People said to us 'You're young, you'll have other children'
but that doesn't bring back our Josh,
Our beloved first-born son.
Our family will never be complete again,
There will always be a hole in my heart.
I know their words are well meant but all I hear are empty
clichés.
His death, the death of all of those children was a needless
waste; it achieved nothing.

So many murders so that one child could be eliminated –
except apparently, he wasn't.
There is no sense, my pain is endless, my tears will flow forever.
Where was God in all of this?
I struggle to hang on to my faith.

15. Simeon

I've seen lots of babies over the years, of course I have; I'm an old man.

I've seen numerous proud parents bringing their first-born sons to the temple to dedicate them to God.

You will rightly ask me what was so special about that morning? What made that baby stand out from all of the others? Why did I have such a clear sense of what he was to become?
And of the mixture of joy and sorrow it would bring his mother?

Of course, it was all strange, irrational.

How could I have discerned so much from the face of a child a mere forty days old?

I hadn't come to the temple expecting anything out of the ordinary, and yet I knew I had to be there, God's Spirit had prompted me.

Some people talk about coincidence; I prefer to talk in terms of God instances-
The right people in the right place at the right time.

If I'd gone to the temple a day earlier or a day later, I would have missed them,
But God's timing is perfect.
I still can't get over what happened: I'm the happiest man alive.

As I looked into the eyes of the child held lovingly by his mother it suddenly dawned on me, he was the personification of all my hopes, my years of yearning and longing.

This child, not yet two months old, was the fulfilment of God's ancient promises.

I had glimpsed the salvation God had prepared for His chosen people Israel. This very ordinary looking baby was the promised saviour.

And yet I also 'saw' the inconceivable, he was to widen people's understanding of God's love and purposes for he would be no nationalistic Messiah. He would also be the light to enlighten the gentiles, the non-Jews.

I somehow felt disloyal, unpatriotic about voicing that and yet I knew it was true. I realised for centuries we had limited God, we had set parameters around His love.

Then, emboldened, I spoke to his mother.

I'm still not sure whether it was the best course of action for it was a two-edged sword and yet I knew it would prove to be true.

The one who would grow up to bring light and glory, the one who would embody God's salvation would be rejected and his mother's heart would be pierced. Joy and sorrow inextricably intertwined.

He would not be the type of Messiah people were expecting and hoping for. The child I held in my arms would not become a Warrior King. He would, so to speak, upset the religious apple cart. He would show the universality of God's love.

The baby was vulnerable, he was dependent on the love and protection of those around him.

Could it be the Messiah, God's agent of salvation would also be vulnerable, would actually need other people?

It was an extraordinary encounter, an unexpected epiphany.

I am a happy, fulfilled old man ready to depart this life in peace having seen his hopes fulfilled. God has been faithful to me.

16. Following a Dead Star? Get A Life!

The new star, seen at its dawning was a very old star, dead
for millions of years.
Its brightness only a distant memory of its previous glory.
Strange to be so excited by something that no longer exists,
To follow a star that seemed to be moving
But had long since moved to its annihilation.
A parallel universe; the timelessness of time,
The unreality of apparent reality.

With our sophisticated knowledge and scientific
instruments
We laugh at their limited wisdom, those so called wise men.
Our godlike telescope, fruit of the tree of knowledge
Redefines the universe, reality, all that is.

But they made the journey, they took the risk.
They left their homes; their comfort; their reputations
And set off.
They found what they were looking for
Although it wasn't what they had expected to find.
Did they laugh or cry on their arrival
Or were they simply exhausted and just relieved to be there?

How embarrassing as they surveyed their surroundings
And looked at their inappropriate, incongruous gifts
Which had seemed so right when they set off
And during all those long, tortuous miles
When they had cursed the weight and the bulk of the gifts
they bore.
But now, as they looked at the child a new reality dawned.
What could they give in the presence of the one who is the
ultimate and eternal gift,
The supreme giver of all gifts?

But they had brought their gifts and they would give them.
And then what?

What would they tell the people in their own country
when they returned
Those who had been astonished at the concept of the
journey?
Would the wise men have become laughing stocks,
Investing so much time and effort to visit a child of
humble parentage?
How could they explain that it really wasn't like that?
That you had to have been there to know the reality, a
reality that defied words and reason.
Their world was no longer as they thought it had been,
Their wisdom challenged and undermined,
A new reality born, revealed by a dead star pointing to a
living, life giving God.

Turning the busyness of Christmas preparations into opportunities for prayer

The run up to Christmas is a busy period with lots of demands on our time and attention.

The commercial world reminds us of how many shopping days are left before Christmas, why don't Christians ask how many praying days are left before Christmas?

We needn't be afraid to fully enter into society's celebration of Christmas, remember, Christmas is about God fully immersing Himself in the world. Use your activities as a springboard for prayer.

As you write your Christmas cards spend a while thinking about the person / people that card is for. Recall their circumstances and hold them before God in prayer.

Choose your presents carefully and with love rather than in a perfunctory way so that each present may be a blessing to the recipient.

Pray for those who will receive no cards or presents.

As you put up your Christmas lights and decorate your home making it feel festive, pray for those who have little light or joy in their lives.

As you prepare for parties, give thanks for friends, fun, laughter and all God's goodness. Pray for those who will be spending Christmas alone or separated from their loved ones.

As you raise a glass and say 'Cheers' pray for those whose lives are marred by alcohol - alcoholics and their families.

As you come in out of the cold and gather round a blazing fire (or at least into a warm heated room) pray for those who are homeless; all who will be sleeping rough at Christmas. Ask God's blessing on all charities and organisations giving them a Christmas dinner and a bed for the night. Could you give them a donation over Christmas?

As you tuck into your Christmas lunch pray for those who will have nothing to eat over Christmas and for all those dependent on food banks. Could you support them in some way?

As we hear again the message of the angels of peace and goodwill, pray for those who live in places beset by war, conflict and violence.
How could you be a messenger of peace, goodwill and reconciliation?

As you go to church, sing carols and celebrate the birth of Jesus pray for those who do not, or cannot, believe in him.

Posada – Offering Hospitality for the night

Posada is a simple but meaningful Christmas tradition taken from South American culture. The word Posada means an inn or shelter.

The way in which it's kept in our country involves figures of Mary and Joseph 'travelling' between 16th and 24th December and staying overnight in a different home each night.

Why the nine days up to Christmas Eve? That's the time it would have taken Mary and Joseph to make the journey from Nazareth to Bethlehem.

People are invited to host Mary and Joseph for the night before helping them on their journey to their next resting place. It's a lovely way of involving people of all ages in preparing for Christmas; even better when on occasions Mary and Joseph are offered a night's stay in a care home or school or pub. It's a simple thing but it reminds us of the precariousness of Mary and Joseph's journey and it's a good way of symbolically welcoming God into our homes and institutions; making a place for Him in our crowded lives.

Of course it's easy to find room in our homes for small wooden, ceramic or knitted figures for the night but surely they remind us of a more challenging question.

How willing are we to show a welcome to unmarried mothers, to those who are homeless, to those who are refugees in the 'real world'?

It's relatively easy to be generous, to exude peace and goodwill over the Christmas season, but isn't part of the challenge of Christmas to live that way always?

Some pointers for reflection, prayer, or discussion if you are part of a group

Celebrating Christmas

1. It is often said that Christmas in our country has become too commercialized: what do you think?

2. How do you think Christians should balance their celebration of Christmas with the recognition that we live in a predominantly secular society?

3. What do you think about referring to Christmas as 'The Winter Festival' to avoid causing offence to non-Christians?

4. How important do you think it is that children are taught the Christmas story in school?

5. What do you think is the most effective way in which churches can share the message of Christmas with those who don't normally attend?

6. What do you think Jesus might think about the way in which we celebrate his birth?

7. What is the highlight of your celebration of Christmas?

Advent and Christmas

1. What do you think is the purpose and value of the season of Advent if any?

2. We make lots of practical preparations for our celebration of Christmas: do you make any spiritual preparations for the observance of Christmas?

3. In the church's calendar there are clear seasons that evoke different moods and feelings. What contribution do you think variety and changes in rhythm contribute to the Christian year?

4. What are your views about singing Christmas carols in Advent?

5. What is your favourite Christmas carol? Can you explain why?

Characters from the Christmas Story

1. What characters from the Christmas story do you find it easiest and hardest to identify with? Why is this?

2. If the Christmas story was to happen again in our world here and now where do you think it would be set and who do you think would be the main characters?

3. God communicated the birth of Jesus through angels. How do you think He would communicate such momentous news now?

4. Who do you think would be the first to hear the good news?

Presents

1. What is the best Christmas present you ever received? What made it special?

2. How do you choose Christmas presents for other people?

3. Why do you think God gave humanity the gift of Himself born as a baby?

4. What present may you wish to give God?

5. What presents do you think give God the greatest joy?

Listening to the Angels

Angels and dreams figure significantly in the Christmas story

Appearing to Zechariah in the temple and telling him his wife Elizabeth would have a son

Announcing to Mary that she was favoured in God's sight and would bear his son

Appearing to Joseph in a dream telling him not to be afraid to take Mary as his wife as she had conceived by the Holy Spirit

Appearing to the shepherds out in the fields giving them the message of peace, good will and the birth of a saviour in a stable at Bethlehem.

Joseph had a dream telling him to escape to Egypt with Mary and the young child Jesus

Do you think God still communicates through angels and dreams?

Have we lost the ability to hear them? How might we improve our listening skills and tune in to God's communication?

How do you think God communicates with you?

The Joy of Christmas

Christmas is a celebration of God's love and God's commitment to us and all people. It's a reminder of that amazing truth that He is Emmanuel, God with us and God for us, wherever, whenever, whatever, no ifs or buts and no exceptions. God with us and God for us, period.

He is there with us in our sadness as well as our joys; in our failures as well as our successes; in our fears as well as our hopes, our sickness as well as our health, and yes in death as well as in birth. Wherever we are, He is. He has come to be with us. But he didn't just come as a visitor, He came to stay. St John in the wonderfully profound prologue to his gospel says 'The Word became flesh and dwelt among us'. A modern version of the Bible puts it like this 'The Word became flesh and blood and moved into the neighbourhood'. In other words, God made His home with us because He wanted to be where we are.

That is the good news of Christmas. God didn't have to do this. He could have continued sending messengers to tell us He loved us and how much we matter to Him, but no, He came Himself and showed us: God with us, God for us and God alongside us.

But as St John tells us he didn't just come to those who welcomed Him. He comes to everyone, even to those people we find it hard to understand and difficult to like. He comes to those places where we wouldn't go and where we wouldn't consider looking for him.

He who was born as a baby and laid in an animal's feeding trough because that was the best place his poor, exhausted, unmarried parents could find for him, this same Jesus is to be found in the drug re-hab centre; in the solitary confinement cell of the maximum security prison; in the dehumanizing and degrading asylum reception centre; in the overcrowded and insanitary refugee camps; in the shop doorways and park benches where the homeless out of sight out of mind community of our country live, here and in countless other places like them, He makes His home.

Does that surprise us? Does that shock us? Surely it shouldn't for as we sing 'With the poor and mean and lowly, lived on earth our saviour holy'. Of course, He comes to each and every human being but perhaps most especially to those who need him most and those who recognize him least.

That may surprise us, for that is not the way we tend to do things, but what is more amazing is that God came at all.

God the creator of all things the one without whom nothing could have existed became a creature. God who is eternal, who is outside of time chose to be born in time, God who is Spirit and is present everywhere chose to subject Himself to the constraints of space and place, God who is immortal chose to be born, God whose glory fills the heavens chose to be held in a manger, an animals' feeding trough. That is truly amazing and surprising.

That should surprise us, that should shock us, but that is what God is like. That is what He has done to show beyond a shadow of doubt the nature and the magnitude of His love.

He was and remains God with us and God for us and 'Where meek souls will receive Him, still the dear Christ enters in'.

About the Author

The Revd Alison J Askew is a retired priest in the Anglican Diocese of Leeds. For twenty years she served as a whole time hospital chaplain in Hampshire and for ten years as a parish priest in rural North Yorkshire. In 2020 she took early retirement to become full time carer for her elderly mother.

Alison has co-led seven pilgrimages to The Holy Land in the last twelve years and has made visits on her own to support and encourage Palestinian friends and charities. She is involved with a number of smaller charities in Bethlehem and Bethany some of which she has been instrumental in establishing, as well as supporting existing better known charities.

During the last couple of years she has felt privileged to be invited to lead worship once or twice a month at the small chapel of St Mary Magdalen in Ripon.

Alison is author of 'The People of the Passion' also published by New Generation Publishing.

Lightning Source UK Ltd.
Milton Keynes UK
UKHW040606201022
410791UK00005B/219

9 781803 695297